Get pupils' knowledge in order with CGP!

Looking for a simple way to help pupils learn all the key facts for Year 6 Science?
Well, look no further — this Knowledge Organiser is the perfect solution!

We've condensed each topic down to the key facts, so it covers
exactly what pupils need, with clear diagrams and tables.

And that's not all! There's a matching Year 6 Science Knowledge Retriever — a
great way of making sure pupils have got to grips with the facts on every page.

CGP – still the best! ☺

Our sole aim here at CGP is to produce the highest quality books —
carefully written, immaculately presented and dangerously close to being funny.

Then we work our socks off to get them out to you
— at the cheapest possible prices.

Published by CGP.

Editors: Josie Gilbert, Jake McGuffie, Luke Molloy, Rachael Rogers, Charlotte Sheridan and George Wright

Contributors: Paddy Gannon, Philip Goodyear, Tony Laukaitis and Lesley Lockhart

With thanks to Glenn Rogers and Jamie Sinclair for the proofreading.

With thanks to Jan Greenway for the copyright research.

ISBN: 978 1 78908 954 7

Printed by Elanders Ltd, Newcastle upon Tyne.

Clipart from Corel®

Illustrations by: Sandy Gardner Artist, email sandy@sandygardner.co.uk

Based on the classic CGP style created by Richard Parsons.

Contents

Classification

Reasons for Classification

Classification means putting living things into groups based on the features they share.

We classify living things to make them easier to identify and study.

Animals:
- Can't make their own food.
- Can move around.

Invertebrates
(animals without a backbone)

Vertebrates
(animals with a backbone)

Micro-organisms:
- Are extremely small (e.g. bacteria).

Plants:
- Can make their own food.
- Are fixed in the ground.

Non-flowering

Flowering

Living things

Plants

Non-flowering

Coniferous trees
Have cones instead of flowers, and keep their leaves in winter.

Mosses
Often grow in shady areas.

Algae
Often grow in ponds.

Flowering

Deciduous trees
Lose their leaves in winter.

Shrubs

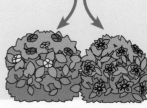

Invertebrates

Spiders

Two body parts

Eight legs

Worms

No legs or antennae

Snails and Slugs

Shell

Slimy foot

Insects

Three body parts

Six legs

Vertebrates

Fish

Breathe with gills

Goby

Carp

Fins and scales

Birds

Parrot

Wings

Feathers

Ostrich

Mammals

Human

Body hair or fur

Dog

Mammals give birth to live babies.

Cereals

Grasses

Reptiles

Lizard

Dry and scaly skin

Lay eggs on land

Cobra

Amphibians

Damp skin

These are born with gills, but develop lungs.

Salamander

Lay eggs in water

Frog

The Circulatory System

The Circulatory System

The circulatory system is made up of three parts:

1. **The blood**
2. The blood vessels
3. **The heart**

The Role of the Blood

The blood carries substances around the body.

The Role of Blood Vessels

Blood vessels are found all over the body, and the blood circulates (travels) through them.

There are three types of blood vessel:

Type	Function
Arteries	Carry blood away from the heart.
Veins	Carry blood back to the heart.
Capillaries	Where substances move in and out of the blood.

The Role of the Heart

The heart pumps blood through the blood vessels:

1 Artery carries blood to the lungs, where it picks up oxygen.

2 Vein brings the blood back.

When the heart beats, it pumps blood out of both arteries.

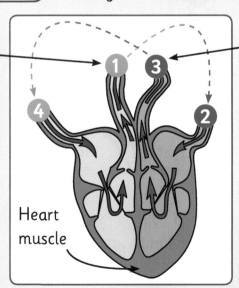

Heart muscle

3 Artery carries blood with oxygen to all parts of the body.

4 Vein brings the blood without oxygen back, and the cycle repeats.

Transportation of Substances

The body takes in:

- **oxygen** — from air (via the lungs)
- **nutrients** — from food
- **water**

↓

The blood carries them around the whole body.

↓

Our body parts use them for energy, and give waste substances **to the blood**.

This is how nutrients and water are transported in other animals too.

The blood carries the waste to the lungs and kidneys to be removed.

Diet, Exercise and Drugs

Diet

We get **nutrients** from the food we eat.

↓

We need to eat the **right amount** of each nutrient to stay healthy.

↓

We can do this by eating a balanced diet.

Exercise

Exercise is important for keeping the body healthy.

It strengthens your muscles, heart and lungs.

It can prevent the body getting fat by using up food for energy.

Nutrients	Why they're needed	Which foods have them
Carbohydrates **(Starches)**	For energy.	Bread, pasta, potatoes
Carbohydrates **(Sugars)**		Sweets, cakes, biscuits
Fats		Meat, dairy, oils
Vitamins and minerals	For healthy cells.	Fruit, vegetables, dairy
Proteins	For growth and repair.	Meat, fish, nuts, beans
Water	To live.	Drinks (plus some foods)
Fibre	To help food move through the gut.	Fruit, vegetables, wholegrain bread

It improves your co-ordination.

It can help you sleep at night.

How regular exercise helps the body

Drugs are dangerous if misused.

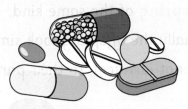

They can be addictive, and can cause a lot of damage to the brain and body.

Alcohol

Can raise blood pressure

Can damage the liver, heart and stomach

Slows your reactions

Solvents

Can cause brain damage

They are addictive

Solvents are chemicals commonly found in everyday products, such as paint and glue.

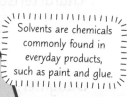

Smoking

Tobacco contains nicotine, which is addictive.

Can cause heart attacks, blocked arteries, cancer and breathing issues.

Animals Including Humans   7

Variation and Adaptations

Variation

Animals and plants produce **offspring** of the same kind. Usually the offspring look similar, but not identical, to their parents.

Father:
brown eyes

We look like our parents because we **inherit** some characteristics from them.

Daughter:
brown eyes

Adaptations

Animals and plants can develop **adaptations** (special features) to suit the place they live in. Adaptations help living things survive in their environment.

Animal Adaptations — Examples

Name: Penguin

Environment: South Pole (cold, wet, icy)

webbed feet
help them swim

We look different to our parents because we have some characteristics that are different from them. These differences are called **variation**.

Mother

Father

Son

different hair shade

different face shape

For example, animals living in or near a pond might have developed features like:

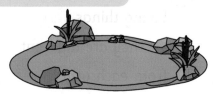

camouflage to help them hide in the reeds

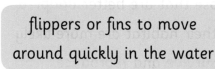

flippers or fins to move around quickly in the water

gills to breathe underwater

rounded body shape reduces heat loss

don't produce much wee or sweat to save water

Name: Camel
Environment: Desert (hot, dry, sandy)

sandy colour for camouflage

layer of body fat keeps them warm

big feet to stop them sinking into the sand

Plant Adaptations — Examples

Name: Cactus
Environment: Desert (hot, dry, sandy)

Name: Moth Orchid
Environment: Jungle (hot, wet, humid)

waxy, waterproof leaves to avoid rot

bright flowers to attract insects

thin needle leaves don't lose water

fleshy stems store water

long roots find water

Evolution

How Living Things Evolve

Evolution is how living things change over time:

1 Living things vary — they are different from each other.

2 Those that are better adapted to their habitat are more likely to survive and reproduce.

3 Many of the offspring will inherit the useful adaptations.

4 Over time, more and more of the living things will have the features that make them well-adapted to their habitat.

Example: How Giraffes Evolved

1 A long time ago, a group of giraffe-like animals existed. Some had longer necks than others.

2 The animals with longer necks could reach more leaves to eat, so were more likely to survive and have babies.

Fossils

Fossils are the shapes of long dead plants and animals that can be found in rocks.

Fossils form when the remains of dead plants and animals get trapped in mud and sand that turns into rock. This takes a very long time.

Plants and animals around today look different from those that were around millions of years ago. This is because they have evolved over time.

Fossils can show us what some plants and animals used to look like. E.g.:

fossil

animal alive today

The fossil shows that the animal alive today has evolved to have longer legs and a more rounded body.

3

Many of the babies inherited their parents' longer necks, which helped them to survive too.

4

This process carried on until eventually the animals had evolved into giraffes, which all have long necks.

Evolution and Inheritance   11

Light, Reflection and Shadows

How Light Travels

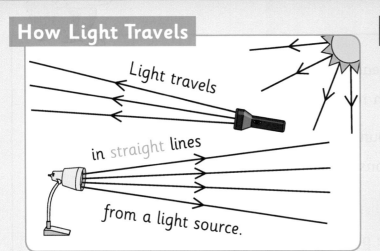

Light travels in straight lines from a light source.

How We See Things

We see things when light enters our eyes.

Shadows

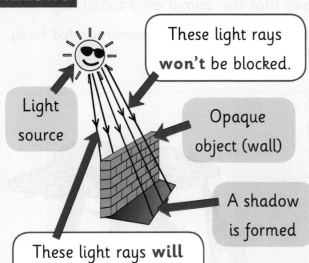

These light rays **won't** be blocked.

Light source

Opaque object (wall)

A shadow is formed

These light rays **will** be blocked by the wall.

When the Sun is lower in the sky, the shadow will be longer.

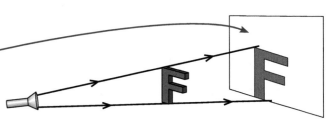

Because light travels in straight lines, shadows are the **same** shape as the objects that cast them.

Light reflects off objects so we can see them.

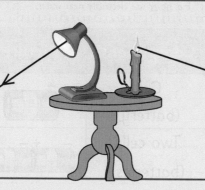

Light can also come directly from the light source.

Mirrors

Mirrors reflect light rays back at the same angle. This can be useful if you want to see around objects.

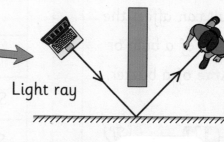

Light ray

Reflected light ray

Patrick

Light ray

Mirror 1

Periscopes like this have two mirrors. Submarines use them to see things above the water.

The closer a light source is to an object, the larger the shadow.

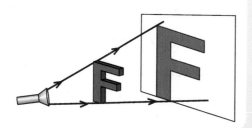

Mirror 2

Circuits and Components

Circuit Symbols

Circuit diagrams use **symbols** instead of pictures.

Electricity can be very dangerous, so you need to work safely with it. E.g. <u>never</u> use electricity near water.

Component	Picture	Symbol
Cell (battery)		
Two cells (batteries)		
Bulb		
Buzzer		
Motor		
Switch (off)		
Switch (on)		

Changes in Circuits

Changing the components in a circuit can affect the **brightness** of a bulb or the **volume** of a buzzer.

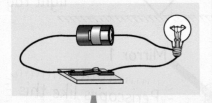

1

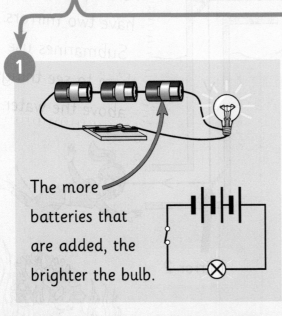

The more batteries that are added, the brighter the bulb.

2

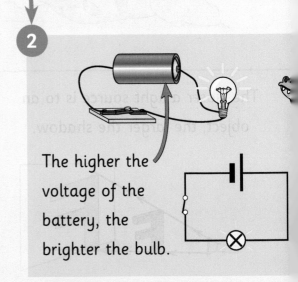

The higher the voltage of the battery, the brighter the bulb.

Here's a picture of a circuit:

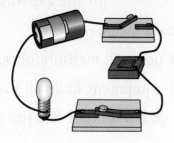

Here's the same circuit shown as a circuit diagram:

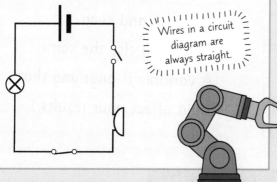

Wires in a circuit diagram are always straight.

A buzzer would get louder or quieter in the same ways.

3 The more bulbs that are added, the dimmer each bulb becomes.

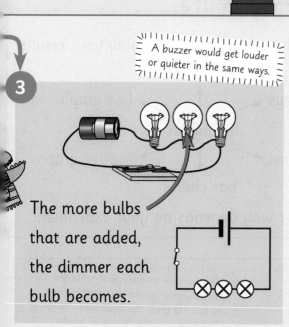

Switches control the flow of electricity in a circuit.

A closed switch completes the circuit so electricity can flow.

For electricity to flow, the circuit also needs to have no other gaps and a power source such as a battery.

An open switch creates a gap in the circuit so electricity can't flow.

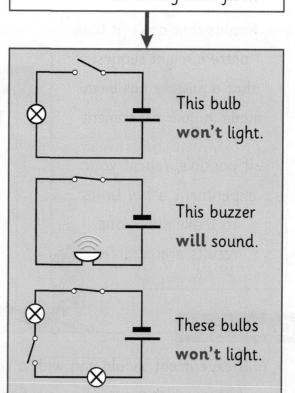

This bulb **won't** light.

This buzzer **will** sound.

These bulbs **won't** light.

Working Scientifically

Planning an Experiment

1. Write down the question you want to answer.

2. Write a method for the experiment. This should include:
   - what you will measure/observe,
   - what equipment you will use,
   - how you will make it a fair test.

   To make an experiment fair, change one **variable** at a time and keep everything else the same. (A variable is anything that could affect your results.)

Patterns in Results

Your results may form a pattern. E.g.:

Distance (cm)	Width of shadow (cm)
20	19
40	20
60	24
80	21

Results that don't fit the pattern might suggest that a mistake has been made in your experiment.

If possible, repeat your experiment a few times to make sure your results are reliable.

Displaying Results

Think about how best to display your results.

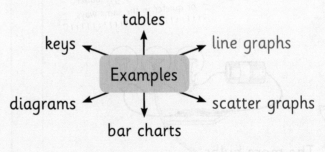

keys → tables → line graphs
Examples
diagrams → bar charts → scatter graphs

The best way depends on your experiment.

Conclusions

Your experiment should end with a conclusion — a sentence that sums up your findings.

The sentence is usually written like: 'As one thing changes like this, another thing changes like this.' You could back this up by using examples from your results.

3 Make a prediction
(what you think will happen).

Line Graphs

Plot your results on a grid, then join them up with straight lines.

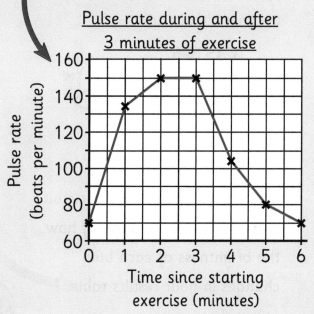

Pulse rate during and after 3 minutes of exercise

Pulse rate (beats per minute) vs Time since starting exercise (minutes)

Line graphs are often used to show how something changes over time.

Scatter Graphs

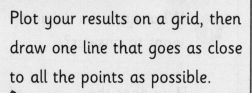

Plot your results on a grid, then draw one line that goes as close to all the points as possible.

Width of an object's shadow for different distances between the object and screen

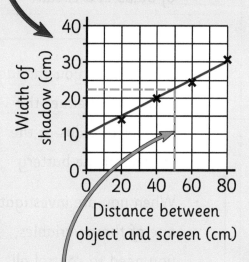

Width of shadow (cm) vs Distance between object and screen (cm)

By drawing from the x-axis to the line, then across to the y-axis, you can predict the width of the shadow for different distances, e.g.: 'The shadow will be 23 cm wide at a distance of 50 cm.'

Explain whether there were any problems with your experiment:

· Did you make any mistakes?
· Did all the results fit with the pattern?
· Could the test have been more fair?

Problems with the experiment might mean your results are not reliable — if so, you might want to do further tests.

Investigation – Changing Circuits

Planning your Experiment

1 What question do you want to answer?

How does the number of bulbs or the voltage of a battery affect the brightness of bulbs in a circuit?

- The variable you change each time is either the number of bulbs <u>or</u> the voltage of the battery.

- When you are investigating one of these variables, you need to control all the other variables.

- The variable you observe is the brightness of the bulb (or bulbs).

2 How will you do your experiment?

1. Make the circuit shown below and observe the brightness of the bulb. This is the original circuit that you will compare the brightness of bulbs in other circuits to.

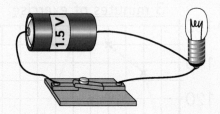

2. Add another bulb to your circuit. Record your observation of how the brightness of each bulb changes in your results table.

You could change the circuit back and forth with the original to make your comparison of the brightness more accurate.

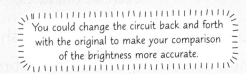

3. Repeat step 2 for the different changes to the circuit that you're investigating — adding different numbers of bulbs and changing the voltage of the battery.

Change to original circuit	Observations compared to original circuit
1 extra bulb added	each bulb is dimmer
2 extra bulbs added	each bulb is dimmer — bulbs are a bit dimmer than when 1 extra bulb was added
3 extra bulbs added	each bulb is dimmer — bulbs are a bit dimmer than when 2 extra bulbs were added
1.5 V battery changed to 4.5 V	bulb is quite a lot brighter than before
1.5 V battery changed to 7.5 V	bulb was very bright for a moment, then went out

You might come up with further predictions based on your results, which you could test by doing another experiment. E.g. you might predict that to make the bulb brighter, you could add more batteries instead of using a more powerful one.

This result doesn't fit with the pattern — you might want to repeat the experiment to see if it happens again.

3 What do you predict will happen?

Increasing the number of bulbs in the circuit will reduce the brightness of each bulb, but increasing the voltage of the battery will increase the brightness.

Conclusion

The results show:
- the more bulbs there are, the dimmer each bulb is.
- the higher the voltage of the battery, the brighter the bulb is.

Glossary

Adaptation	A characteristic of an organism that helps it to survive in its habitat.
Alcohol	A drug that's found in some drinks like wine and beer. If you drink too much it can damage your heart, liver and stomach.
Artery	A blood vessel which carries blood away from the heart.
Balanced diet	This means eating the right amount of different nutrients to stay healthy.
Blood	The red liquid that transports nutrients, water and oxygen around the body, as well as waste products.
Capillary	A blood vessel where substances move in and out of the blood.
Characteristic	A feature of an organism. For example, freckles are a characteristic of some humans.
Circuit diagram	A picture that uses circuit symbols to show all the components in a circuit and how they're connected.
Circulatory system	The system that transports substances around the body in the blood.
Classification	When living things are put into groups based on their features.
Component	Something that does a job in a circuit, e.g. a bulb or a buzzer.
Conclusion	A simple sentence that sums up what you found out in an experiment.
Drug	A substance that changes how the body works.
Evolution	How living things change over time.
Fair test	An experiment where only one variable is changed, and all other variables are controlled (kept the same).
Fossil	The shape of a long dead animal or plant, found in a rock.

Habitat	Where an organism <u>lives</u>.
Heart	The organ that <u>pumps</u> blood around the body.
Inheritance	When <u>characteristics</u> get passed on from a <u>parent</u> to its <u>offspring</u>.
Invertebrate	An animal without a <u>backbone</u>.
Light ray	A beam of <u>light</u>. Light always travels in <u>straight lines</u>.
Light source	Something that gives out its <u>own light</u>.
Micro-organism	An <u>extremely small</u> living thing, e.g. bacteria.
Nutrients	Substances that a plant or animal needs to <u>live</u> and <u>grow</u>.
Offspring	The <u>children</u> of a living thing.
Prediction	What you think will <u>happen</u> in an <u>experiment</u>.
Reflection	When light <u>bounces off</u> a surface.
Shadow	A <u>dark</u> area made when light rays are <u>blocked</u> by an object.
Solvent (drug)	Substances that you inhale, e.g. glues and paints, which can be <u>addictive</u> and can damage your brain.
Tobacco	A substance found in cigarettes and cigars. It contains <u>nicotine</u>, which is <u>addictive</u>. Smoking it can cause <u>health problems</u>.
Variable	A <u>factor</u> in an experiment that you can <u>control</u>, <u>change</u> or <u>measure</u>.
Variation	<u>Differences</u> between living things.
Vein	A <u>blood vessel</u> that takes blood <u>back</u> to the heart.
Vertebrate	An animal with a <u>backbone</u>.
Voltage	A measure of the amount of <u>power</u> something has. For example, the <u>higher</u> the <u>voltage</u> of a battery, the <u>more power</u> it has.

Index